Encounters with God

The Epistle of JAMES

Encounters with God

The Epistle of JAMES

CONTENTS

AN INTRODUCTION
TO THE EPISTLE OF JAMES

This study guide covers the epistle of James. It is considered to be a General Epistle, which means that its message was written to all believers, not only those in one particular church. There is strong indication that this letter may have been the first New Testament book to have been written. James, the brother of Jesus and the pastor of the first church in Jerusalem, is generally recognized as the author.

In many ways, the book of James is like the book of Proverbs in that it offers practical, moral, and ethical instructions. The illustrations are simple and vivid. The book calls Christians to righteous living and offers down-to-earth and readily-applied teaching on how to deal with temptation, curb the tongue, pray with effective power, and demonstrate faith through acts of kindness. The tone and content of James is that of a teacher seeking to disciple followers.

In the opening line of the letter, James referred to the "twelve tribes which are scattered abroad" (James 1:1). This reference is likely a figurative description of a distinctly Jewish body of Christians who had been dispersed among the unbelieving nations in the aftermath of persecution. Historical events in the first century forced many Jews to flee their homeland of Judea and settle in areas where the gospel had not yet been preached. James desired that those believers—some of whom were former members of the congregation in Jerusalem—would stay on course in their faith. He wrote hoping they would continue to mature as Christians and to assume full responsibility for their own spiritual progress regardless of cultural pressures. James offered both encouragement and admonition that the believers remain unified in the face of persecution and that they continue to show love to one another. He urges them to seek wisdom from God about how to stand firm in their faith, regardless of the fiery trials that might come their way.

The goal and prevalent theme of the book is the development of an enduring faith.

James is written plainly, with easily understood concepts. The book echoes many of the themes of the Old Testament prophets, encouraging believers to avoid the empty traditions of religious practice and to demonstrate genuine compassion, kindness, and love toward widows, orphans, and strangers. God is presented as being involved in the day-to-day activities and interests of humanity, and as being pleased by even the simplest acts of faith that are expressed with love.

Through the centuries the Book of James has received some criticism from theologians, most notably Martin Luther, who saw in the book a discrepancy with the writings of the apostle Paul. A close study of the book, however, clearly demonstrates theological agreement between James and Paul. Both were writing to a church facing or enduring persecution, and while their perspectives may be slightly different, the core teachings about how to remain firm in faith are the same.

About the Author. James was one of the sons of Joseph and Mary and, thus, the half-brother of Jesus. Like other family members, James did not accept the claims of Christ until after the Resurrection (1 Corinthians 15:7). He eventually became the elder of the church in Jerusalem and was respected as a leader throughout the network of early churches for his role in the Jerusalem Council (Acts 15:6–11).

According to the Jewish historian Josephus, James was martyred in A.D. 62, so the book was written prior to that date. It may have been written as early as A.D. 48, shortly before the meeting of the Jerusalem Council described in Acts 15. The book describes a simple church structure of teachers and elders who met in synagogues or assemblies; this form of church organization was prominent among the Jerusalem believers between A.D. 46 and 60. While the exact year of writing is uncertain, all of these factors point toward the book being composed between A.D. 48 and 60. It was probably written from Jerusalem.

AN OVERVIEW OF OUR STUDY OF THE EPISTLE OF JAMES

This study guide presents seven lessons drawn from the epistle of James and elaborating upon the commentary included in the *Blackaby Study Bible*:

Lesson #1: Facing Trials and Temptations

Lesson #2: Becoming Doers of the Word

Lesson #3: The Relationship Between Faith and Works

Lesson #4: Power in What We Say

Lesson #5: Wisdom in Relationships

Lesson #6: Confronting Self

Lesson #7: Healing for All Who Are Suffering

Personal or Group Use. These lessons are offered for personal study and reflection or for small-group Bible study. The questions may be answered by an individual reader or used as a foundation for group discussion. A segment titled "Notes to Leaders of Small Groups" is included at the back of this book to help those leading a group study of this material.

Before you embark on this study, we encourage you to read in full the statement in the *Blackaby Study Bible* titled "How to Study the Bible." Our contention is that the Bible is unique among all literature. It is God's definitive word for humanity. The Bible is

- *inspired*—"God-breathed"

- *authoritative*—absolutely the final word on any spiritual matter

- *the plumb line of truth*—the standard against which all human activity and reasoning must be evaluated

The Bible is fascinating in that it has remarkable diversity but also remarkable unity. Its books were penned by a diverse assortment of authors representing a variety of languages and cultures, and it contains a number of literary forms. But the Bible's message, from cover to cover, is clear, consistent, and unified.

More than mere words on a page, the Bible is an encounter with God himself. No book is more critical to your life. The very essence of the Bible is the Lord himself.

The Holy Spirit speaks through the Bible. He also communicates during your time of prayer, in your life circumstances, and through the church. Read your Bible in an attitude of prayer, and allow the Holy Spirit to make you aware of God's activity in and through your personal life. Write down what you learn, meditate on it, and adjust your thoughts, attitudes, and behavior accordingly. Look for ways every day to apply the truth of God's Word to your circumstances and relationships. God is not random; He is orderly and intentional in the way He speaks to you.

Be encouraged—the Bible is *not* too difficult for the average person to understand if that person asks the Holy Spirit for help. (Furthermore, not even the most brilliant person can fully understand the Bible apart from the Holy Spirit's help!) God desires for you to know Him and to know His Word. Every person who reads the Bible can learn from it. The person who will receive *maximum* benefit from reading and studying the Bible, however, is the person who:

- *is born again* (John 3:3, 5). Those who are born again and have received the gift of His Spirit have a distinct advantage in understanding the deeper truths of God's Word.

- *has a heart that desires to learn God's truth.* Your attitude greatly influences the outcome of Bible study. Resist the temptation to focus on what others have said about the Bible. Allow the Holy Spirit to guide you as you study God's Word for yourself.

- *has a heart that seeks to obey God.* The Holy Spirit teaches the most to those who desire to apply what they learn.

Begin your Bible study with prayer, asking the Holy Spirit to guide your thoughts and to impress upon you what is on God's heart. Then, make plans to adjust your life to immediately obey the Lord fully.

As you read and study the Bible, your purpose is not to *create* meaning, but to *discover* the meaning of the text with the Holy Spirit's guidance. Ask yourself, "What did the author have in mind? How was this applied by those who first heard these words?" Especially in your study of the Gospel accounts, pay attention to the words of Jesus that begin "truly, truly" or "He opened His mouth and taught them saying." These are core principles and teachings that have powerful impact on *every* person's life.

At times you may find it helpful to consult other passages of the Bible (made available in the center columns in the *Blackaby Study Bible*), or the commentary that is in the margins of the *Blackaby Study Bible*.

Keep in mind always that Bible study is not primarily an exercise for acquiring information but an opportunity for transformation. Bible study is your opportunity to encounter God and to be changed in His presence. When God speaks to your heart, nothing remains the same. Jesus said, "He who has ears to hear, let him hear" (Matt. 13:9). Choose to have ears that desire to hear!

The B-A-S-I-Cs of Each Study in This Guide. Each lesson in this study guide has five segments, using the word BASIC as an acronym. The word BASIC does not allude to elementary or "simple" but, rather, to "foundational." These studies extend the concepts that are part of the *Blackaby Study Bible* commentary and are focused on key aspects of what it means to be a Christ-follower in today's world. The BASIC acronym stands for:

B = *Bible Focus*. This segment presents the central passage for the lesson and a general explanation that covers the central theme or concern.

A = *Application for Today*. This segment has a story or illustration related to modern-day times, with questions that link the Bible text to today's issues, problems, and concerns.

S = *Supplementary Scriptures to Consider*. In this segment other Bible verses related to the general theme of the lesson are explored.

I = *Introspection and Implications*. In this segment questions are asked that lead to deeper reflection about one's personal faith journey and life experiences.

C = *Communicating the Good News*. In this segment challenging questions point to ways the lesson's truth might be lived out and shared with others, whether to win the lost or build up the church.

LESSON #1

FACING TRIALS
AND TEMPTATIONS

*Patience: the ability to endure waiting, delay, or provocation
without being upset or losing one's temper*

B
Bible Focus

> *My brethren, count it all joy when you fall into various trials, knowing that the testing of your faith produces patience. But let patience have its perfect work, that you may be perfect and complete, lacking nothing. If any of you lacks wisdom, let him ask of God, who gives to all liberally and without reproach, and it will be given to him. But let him ask in faith, with no doubting, for he who doubts is like a wave of the sea driven and tossed by the wind. For let not that man suppose that he will receive anything from the Lord; he is a double-minded man, unstable in all his ways. . . .*
>
> *Blessed is the man who endures temptation; for when he has been approved, he will receive the crown of life which the Lord has promised to those who love him. Let no one say when he is tempted, "I am tempted by God"; for God cannot be tempted by evil, nor does He Himself tempt anyone. But each one is tempted when he is drawn away by his own desires and enticed. Then, when desire has conceived, it gives birth to sin; and sin, when it is full-grown, brings forth death.*
>
> *Do not be deceived, my beloved brethren. Every good gift and every perfect gift is from above, and comes down from the Father of lights, with whom there is no variation or shadow of turning. Of His own will He brought us forth by the word of truth, that we might be a kind of firstfruits of His creatures.*
>
> *So then, my beloved brethren, let every man be swift to hear, low to speak, slow to wrath; for the wrath of man does not produce the righteousness of God.*
>
> *Therefore lay aside all filthiness and overflow of wickedness, and receive with meekness the implanted word, which is able to save your souls. (James 1:2–8, 12–21)*

James opened his letter by dealing with the two big T's that troubled the church then and continue to disturb believers today: Trials and Temptations.

James openly acknowledged that tough times *do* come to good people. No Christian should expect to be immune from going through difficult trials, times of testing, or temptations. To those who might say that Christians *should not* be tested or tempted, James would likely have said, "Get real! There's nothing in one's acceptance of Jesus as Savior or in one's following Jesus as Lord that makes a person exempt from the hardships of this life or rcmoves from a person the natural impulses of their own humanity. We still live in a fallen world and in fallen flesh."

The word James used for "testing" needs to be clearly understood. This word, *peirasmos*, refers to a time of testing that is directed toward a specific intended end. In James' understanding the God-intended end of all testing that comes to a believer is patience, strength and constancy of faith, and ultimately, wholeness or completeness. This Greek word for testing is the same word that is used when a young bird tests its wings as it leaves a nest to fly, and in the Bible it is a word used frequently to describe the struggles Israel faced in order to strengthen the nation. James clearly saw testing as a tremendous benefit in bringing any body of believers to greater maturity and stronger faith. "If you have questions about the reason for your testing," James added quickly, "ask God! He will impart His wisdom to you on the matter, if you ask with faith."

Wisdom, throughout the Bible, is a process of discernment; choices are weighed, options are evaluated. The standard against which all choices and decisions are to be made is the Word of God. To become wise, one must know God's Word and ask God to reveal from his Word the truths and guidance that are vital to any major issue or question a person faces. Part of the process of gaining wisdom is gaining God's perspective on any situation, relationship, or experience. The wise perspective is a perspective that points toward eternal benefit.

Often when people experience a difficult circumstance or season of life, they move first to a concern about what has been lost, is in the process of being lost, or is likely to be lost. Generally speaking, trouble is equated with a potential for failure, damage, or a loss of something considered valuable. "Change your perspective," James seemed to say. "See trouble through the lens of God's wisdom. Testing is a believer's opportunity for growth, refinement, success, and greater enduring power."

James moved quickly from an overview of testing trials to the concept of temptation. Temptations come to every believer, no matter how spiritually mature they may be. Again, temptation has a potential for *good* in a believer's life.

James sought to make it clear that temptations do not come from God. Rather, from James' perspective, they are a natural outflow of mankind's base, fleshly desires. If a person yields to the desires of the flesh—which include psychological issues as well as physical ones—the result is sinful behavior, which encompassed one's thinking and speaking behaviors, as well as one's actions. The end result of sin coming to full-blown fruition is death. Rather than present man with temptations, God gives "every good gift and every perfect gift" that promotes eternal life.

What is a good gift? It is a gift that adds genuine goodness to our lives in a way that allows us to extend good to others.

What is a perfect gift? It is a gift that produces greater spiritual maturity in us and helps us to influence those around us in a way that promotes wholeness. God never undermines His people in any way, either by testing or by temptation. Rather, He always seeks to build up and bless them.

What should be our response to testing trials and temptations? James wrote:

- *be swift to hear*—quickly seek out God's wisdom and heed what God says.

- *be slow to speak*—weigh carefully how you respond to trials.

- *be slow to wrath*—do not become angry at those who cause your troubles or trials.

- *lay aside all filthiness and overflow of wickedness*—continue to live pure lives, refusing to stoop to the level of those who seek your demise.

- *receive with meekness the implanted word*—take all of the wise counsel of God's Word into your life and make it your guide for all decisions and choices.

Do you firmly believe today that God is one hundred percent *for* you and that He does all things for your eternal benefit? If not, why not? If so, cite an example in which you <u>knew</u> God was working on your behalf, even if the prevailing circumstances seemed negative.

Does it make a difference how we approach a problem or difficult circumstance? What role does our attitude have in the ultimate outcome of a difficult time?

A
Application for Today

A Sunday school teacher presented this idea to his class of young adults, most of whom were in their twenties and thirties: "Your greatest heartache will one day be your greatest blessing *if* you turn that heartache over to God." He noted quickly that only one woman in the class seemed to be in full agreement with what he had said. He called upon her, "Do you have a story you would be willing to share with the class about this?"

She said, "When I was twenty-two and about to graduate from college, my fiancé called off our wedding, which was only two weeks away at that time. I was devastated. I had been planning my entire life around marriage to this man and, suddenly, my future was a blank slate. It was a terrible time of heartache to me.

"But I turned it over to God and I felt that I should go to graduate school to get a master's degree. That wasn't an easy choice—it meant more loans and meager living—but I believed it was God's wisdom for me to do this.

"At graduate school I learned about a fellowship program overseas. I applied for it and got a fellowship. It wasn't an easy choice to accept this fellowship. I was in debt, my studies had been very difficult, and I felt exhausted mentally and physically. But again, I felt it was God's wisdom that I take this fellowship. I took out still more loans.

"Once I got overseas I had lots more time than I had anticipated. I poured myself into Bible study, and I attended every Christian seminar I could find in my host nation. Fortunately, there were some good seminars available. It was at one of those seminars that I met a student who was also in that nation on a fellowship. We became good friends, and after we both returned to the United States, we stayed in touch. During the next six months we realized we were in love and we married a year later.

"Was the breakup of my first romance devastating? Yes. It was the hardest thing I had ever gone through. Was graduate school difficult? Yes. It was demanding in ways I never imagined. But those two very difficult experiences set me up for the greatest joys of my life: a marriage to a man I love deeply, an even better career than I would have had with only a bachelor's degree, and a life that is rooted securely in God's Word. If it took the heartache of a breakup to get me grounded in the Bible, there's no putting value on that! If I had to go through that difficult time again to be who I am and to have what I have today, I would do so in the blink of an eye. I can't even imagine being married to the man to whom I was engaged when I was twenty-two. His rejection of me turned out to be a huge blessing."

What about you? Is there a time of testing that God used to build into you things that were and are for your eternal blessing? Has your greatest heartache become your greatest blessing?

S
Supplementary Scriptures to Consider

James believed that the Lord brought just the right "tests" to every person:

> Let the lowly brother glory in his exaltation, but the rich in his humiliation, because as a flower of the field he will pass away. For no sooner has the sun risen with a burning heat than it withers the grass; its flower falls, and its beautiful appearance perishes. So the rich man also will fade away in his pursuits. (James 1:9–11)

• The person low in self-value or from a low socio-economic stratum should never allow trials to reinforce a sense of their low self-worth or poverty. Rather, the "lowly" brother should see his trials as an opportunity for exaltation. Have you ever grown in your confidence in the Lord through a time of difficult testing or trouble? What caused that growth? How did the Lord "lift you up" on the inside as you overcame your time of testing?

• The person who thinks too highly of himself or is from a high socio-economic stratum should never conclude that he is above learning important lessons from difficult circumstances. Rather, the "rich" brother should see his trials as an opportunity to pursue spiritual riches. What lessons have you learned from a time of testing? Especially focus on lessons that might involve a shift in focus from temporal matters to eternal realities.

James addressed our desire to have times of trial or temptation come to a *quick* end:

> Therefore be patient, brethren, until the coming of the Lord. See how the farmer waits for the precious fruit of the earth, waiting patiently for it until it receives the early and latter rain. You also be patient. Establish your hearts, for the coming of the Lord is at hand. (James 5:7–9)

- Have you ever hoped for a "quick fix" to a major problem in your life? What happened? What was the result with regard to your faith?

- Have you ever prayed that God would quickly remove from you an area of weakness that seems particularly prone to temptation? Did God do this? What benefit do you see in the way God responded to your prayer?

- In what ways have you struggled with the concept of patience? Are you a patient person? Are you growing in patience? Why or why not?

- What does the phrase "establish your hearts" mean to you? How does a person do this? What are the benefits of having an established heart?

The apostle Paul wrote this about temptation:

> Let him who thinks he stands take heed lest he fall. No
> temptation has overtaken you except such as is common to
> man; but God is faithful, who will not allow you to be tempted
> beyond what you are able, but with the temptation will also
> make the way of escape, that you may be able to bear it. (1
> Corinthians 10:12–13)

• Have you ever known someone who thought himself impervious to
  temptation or believed she was above being tempted? What happened?

• What is the danger of thinking that you have power to withstand temptation apart from God's help?

• How does a person discover God's "way of escape" when he is tempted?

• Have you ever experienced a divinely provided "way of escape" during a time when you were experiencing temptation? What happened?

James seemed to echo words from Proverbs:

> My son, do not forget my law,
> But let your heart keep my commands;
> For length of days and long life
> And peace they will add to you.
>
> Let not mercy and truth forsake you;
> Bind them around your neck,
> Write them on the tablet of your heart,
> And so find favor and high esteem
> In the sight of God and man.
>
> Trust in the LORD with all your heart,
> And lean not on your own understanding;
> In all your ways acknowledge Him,
> And He shall direct your paths.
>
> Do not be wise in your own eyes;
> Fear the LORD and depart from evil. (Proverbs 3:1–7)

• What stands out to you in a particularly challenging way as you read this passage from Proverbs?

- Recall a time when you know without a shadow of doubt that God directed your path. What happened?

- In what ways do you find it difficult to trust in the Lord with all your heart?

- In what ways do you find it difficult to obey the admonition: "Do not be wise in your own eyes?"

I
Introspection and Implications

1. How do you respond to James' teaching that temptation occurs when a person is "drawn away by his own desires and enticed?" In what ways have you found it difficult to take responsibility for the temptations you experience and for your response to temptations?

2. Have you ever been angry with God for your own yielding to temptation, perhaps saying to God, "You made me this way. How can You expect me to say no to such a temptation?" Do you truly believe God made you with weaknesses so He could trip you up in your weaknesses? To what degree do we make ourselves weaker by repeated yielding to temptation? What aid does God promise us in a time of temptation?

3. Do you always turn *first* to God with a request for wisdom when you experience a difficult time? What do you believe keeps a person from turning to God to ask for wisdom when tough times strike?

4. James wrote that when we turn to God to ask for wisdom, God gives wisdom "liberally and without reproach." In other words, He provides a generous outpouring of wisdom and never berates or belittles us for not already having it. Do you take comfort in this? Have you ever turned to God to ask for specific wisdom on a particular choice, decision, or issue? What happened?

5. Why is it important to ask for wisdom without doubting?

6. Do you value wisdom as highly as you believe you should ? Why or why not?

7. Identify ways you struggle with these admonitions from James:

- be swift to hear —

- be slow to speak—

- be slow to wrath—

- lay aside all filthiness and overflow of wickedness—

- receive with meekness the implanted word—

C
Communicating the Good News

What is the error in focusing an evangelistic message solely on all of the good things that will be given to a person who accepts Jesus as Savior, while neglecting the downside of living in a fallen world and in frail, temptation-prone flesh? Do some evangelists raise expectations too high for a life that is all roses, no thorns? What is the benefit of holding out to a non—Christian the *abiding presence* of Christ Jesus that helps a Christian endure difficult times and overcome temptations?

LESSON #2

BECOMING DOERS OF THE WORD

Integrity: undivided unity in thought, word, and deed, all of which adhere to the highest moral principles

B
Bible Focus

> *Be doers of the word, and not hearers only, deceiving*
> *yourselves. For if anyone is a hearer of the word and not a*
> *doer, he is like a man observing his natural face in a mirror;*
> *for he observes himself, goes away, and immediately forgets*
> *what kind of man he was. But he who looks into the perfect*
> *law of liberty and continues in it, and is not a forgetful hearer*
> *but a doer of the work, this one will be blessed in what he*
> *does. (James 1:22–25)*

James confronted what he perceived to be a tremendous dichotomy between belief and behavior. That dichotomy was not limited to the first century; it is a basic staple of human nature throughout history. People say they believe one way and then act in a totally opposite manner. People advocate for one opinion or give verbal support to one candidate and then vote in favor of the opposing opinion or candidate. People say they believe strongly about an issue and give ardent verbal support to it, and then behave in a way that shows no material or behavioral support—sometimes even acting in a way that is contrary to their stated beliefs.

The person who hears the truth and then fails to live it out does two things *to himself* according to James. First, he deceives himself. He lies to himself and swallows the lie. He thinks himself to be better than he is.

Certainly this would apply to a person who goes to church regularly—even reads his Bible and prays regularly—and thinks he is "just fine" as a Christian. If that person fails to live out what he professes to be true and if he fails to display his relationship to the church and to the Lord in ways that bring honor to both, he is not at all "just fine." He is a going to be regarded as a hypocrite by other people, and he will not be blessed by God.

Second, a person who hears the truth and fails to live it out doesn't really improve himself or grow in his relationship with God and other Christians. In so doing, he undermines his own spiritual potential.

In Bible times mirrors were made from highly polished metal. Still, a person could gain a sense of his own image in such a mirror, certainly observing major blemishes, disheveled hair, and obvious flaws. To look into a mirror and then to fail to correct the imperfection would be to remain less than one's best. It is only in *applying* God's Word to our lives that we truly experience God's best in every area of our life. The authentic Christian life is not a matter of learning theory but of applying practice.

It certainly is important to hear the truth and to believe it. But that's only going halfway. The remaining part of our growing toward wholeness and the full character likeness of Christ is found in living out and declaring the truth, in word and deed, to the world around us that is wallowing in the lies and deception of the devil.

There is an upside to James' admonition: the person who believes and is steadfast in the truth—which James calls the "perfect law of liberty"—and does the work associated with living out God's truth is a person who is going to be *blessed* by God. The "perfect law" is God's revealed will, expressed in love, for the perfection or wholeness of mankind. The perfect law is what points us toward our destiny or purpose on this earth, as individuals and groups of believers. Our obedience to this law brings us to deep inner fulfillment and joy. The "law of liberty" is the law that frees us from the tyranny and slavery of sin and sets us free to *choose* what is God's best and highest for us. Ultimately, the person who accepts, believes, obeys, and pursues a life based upon God's "perfect law of liberty" is a person who is going to experience the highest and best God offers, both now and for all eternity.

In summation:

- Don't lie to yourself!
- Don't refuse to change for the better!
- Don't shortchange yourself or fail to pursue all that God has for you!
- Manifest what you believe in everyday, practical ways.

Have you ever struggled with behaving in ways that were contrary to what you truly believed? Do you currently struggle with an alignment of belief and behavior? In what ways might the Holy Spirit be challenging you to address this misconnect or disconnect in your life and make changes?

A
Application for Today

1. Do you believe it is important to go to church regularly and to get involved in the mission of the church: loving one another, and growing in knowledge and application of the Word of God? Do you go to church regularly? To Sunday school or a regular Bible study? Are you involved in church efforts to build up other believers or to meet practical needs of your fellow parishioners?

2. Do you believe it is important for Christians to give generously to their church? Do you tithe and give offerings?

3. Do you believe it is important to witness to other people about Jesus being the Savior? Are you involved with others in your church in reaching out to unbelievers? Have you shared your faith in Christ Jesus with your next-door neighbors? With your colleagues at work?

4. Do you believe that missionary work and evangelistic work is important? Do you give regularly to missions? Have you been on a short-term mission trip? Have you ever engaged in door-to-door evangelism with others from your church? Are you praying about whether God wants you to go overseas as a missionary?

5. Do you believe that it is important to read your Bible daily and to pray daily? Do you read your Bible every day? Do you pray every day? And now ask: do you believe it is important to be a doer of what you believe?

S
Supplementary Scriptures to Consider

James had strong words to say to those in the church who had the means to help other believers and to reach out to the lost but were not doing the right things they knew to do:

> Come now, you rich, weep and howl for your miseries that are coming upon you! Your riches are corrupted, and your garments are moth-eaten. Your gold and silver are corroded, and their corrosion will be a witness against you and will eat your flesh like fire. You have heaped up treasure in the last days. Indeed the wages of the laborers who mowed your fields, which you kept back by fraud, cry out; and the cries of the reapers have reached the ears of the Lord of Sabaoth. You have lived on the earth in pleasure and luxury; you have fattened your hearts as in a day of slaughter. You have condemned, you have murdered the just; he does not resist you. (James 5:1–6)

• In what ways do the rich oppress the poor in our world today?

- *Sabaoth* is a transliteration of a Hebrew word that means "army." The Lord is head of a powerful angelic army that is poised to defeat those who fail to use their riches to help their brethren. How do you *feel* about the strong language in this passage?

- In what ways do you find it challenging to align your beliefs about money with your behavior in earning, spending, and giving?

James had specific instructions for those who err:

> Brethren, if anyone among you wanders from the truth, and someone turns him back, let him know that he who turns a sinner from the error of his way will save a soul from death and cover a multitude of sins. (James 5:19–20)

- What do you believe is involved in the process of "wandering" from the truth? Is this the result of casual neglect? Is it the result of apathy?

• What is the antidote for wandering from the truth? Can a person stroll toward the truth?

• In what ways do you find it difficult to confront a person about the "error of his way"?

• What happens if a sinner is allowed to continue in error? Does that sinner's error multiply? Do his sins multiply?

I
Introspection and Implications

1. Define "the perfect law of liberty" in your own words, in ways that apply to your own life.

2. In what ways do you find it difficult to look into the perfect law of liberty and then continue in what it is that you see there?

3. How do you keep from being a "forgetful hearer" of God's Word? Be practical in your response!

4. An old adage says: "Say what you mean and mean what you say." How does this apply to James' admonition to be doers of the word? Is what we say a part of being a "doer of the word"?

C
Communicating the Good News

Some people who reject Christianity use "hypocrites in the church" as their excuse. They see a disconnect between what is proclaimed as truth and what is lived out in the real world. How do you respond to this criticism?

Jesus lived a life of total integrity: what He believed matched what He said, which in turn corresponded with what He did. In what ways are we wise to present Jesus as our role model, rather than any other person or institution?

LESSON #3

THE RELATIONSHIP BETWEEN FAITH AND WORKS

Faith: An act of believing what is right

*Work: An act of speaking or doing
what is right before God*

B
Bible Focus

> What does it profit, my brethren, if someone says he has
> faith but does not have works? Can faith save him? If a
> brother or sister is naked and destitute of daily food, and one
> of you says to them, "Depart in peace, be warmed and filled,"
> but you do not give them the things which are needed for the
> body, what does it profit? Thus also faith by itself, if it does
> not have works, is dead.
>
> But someone will say, "You have faith, and I have works."
> Show me your faith without your works, and I will show you
> my faith by my works. You believe that there is one God. You
> do well. Even the demons believe—and tremble! But do you
> want to know, O foolish man, that faith without works is dead?
> Was not Abraham our father justified by works when he
> offered Isaac his son on the altar? Do you see that faith was
> working together with his works, and by works faith was made
> perfect? And the Scripture was fulfilled which says, "Abraham
> believed God, and it was accounted to him for righteousness."
> And he was called the friend of God. You see then that a man
> is justified by works, and not by faith only. (James 2:14–24)

James was speaking against the backdrop of two divergent perspectives
that impacted the first-century church. On the one hand, the Jewish people
had a long history of almsgiving and of doing good works, especially to
widows, orphans, and strangers in their midst. The Jewish church council in
Jerusalem urged Paul to encourage almsgiving among gentile Christians, as
well as Jewish believers (Gal. 2:10). However, in the four hundred years
between the time of the Old Testament prophet Malachi and the coming of
Christ, a number of famous Jewish writers had elevated almsgiving beyond
an act of obedience to the law of Moses (Ex. 22:22 and Deut. 26:12–13).
Ben Sirach wrote: Water will quench a flaming fire, and alms make atone-
ment for sin" (Ecclesiasticus 3:30). The intertestamental book Tobit says,
"Everyone who occupies himself in alms shall behold the face of God, as it
is written, I will behold your face by almsgiving" (Tobit 4:8-10).

The early church rejected all teaching that good works, including almsgiving, could produce salvation or put someone in a special position to behold
God's face in the afterlife. Paul boldly declared, "For by grace you have
been saved through faith, and that not of yourselves; it is the gift of God, not
of works, lest anyone should boast" (Ephesians 2:8–9). Some in the church,
however, interpreted this teaching of salvation by faith alone as freeing them
from all responsibility to do good works. Not so, James said. Those who

have been saved by faith will have an added desire and obligation to display their faith by good works. Works should flow naturally from faith, just as all good behavior should flow from right beliefs.

Second, many of the Jews who had been dispersed by persecution found themselves in a world dominated by Greek thought. One prominent Greek philosophy, Stoicism, rejected all emotion, including the emotion of pity for the poor and compassion for those in need. Under the influence of Greek philosophy, some in the early church began to regard the emotions associated with almsgiving in a negative light, and they shut down their giving even as they closed off their emotions.

In the face of these competing perspectives, many in the early church were suffering and struggling. They had lost their homes, and many had forfeited their families and community affiliation as a result of their faith. Persecuted by nonbelievers, they were also in a real way being persecuted by their fellow believers—those who had the ability to provide practical assistance to them were withholding that aid.

James struck this balance in his teaching:

Works without faith produce nothing that counts for eternity.

Faith without works produces nothing that meets earthly needs.

The two belong together in a dynamic synergy: faith *producing* works, which in turn, give practical life and impetus to greater faith.

James also said this: "Pure and undefiled religion before God and the Father is this: to visit orphans and widows in their trouble, and to keep oneself unspotted from the world" (James 1:27). Note the word *religion*. Religion is the *practice of faith*. It is the work that flows from believing. That work, said James, meant caring for widows and orphans; to visit a person was to show up with practical assistance in hand. True consolation was manifested by alleviating need.

What is the role of almsgiving in your life?

How do you display *works* born of your faith?

A
Application for Today

Those who work in the printing industry apply the word *justify* to typesetting. To justify type is to put text into even columns so letters line up evenly on both the right and left sides of the column. We see this routinely in newspapers. Some lines of text have only a few words, which may seem to be "s p r e a d   o u t" to fill the space. Other lines may have words that seem cramped together. The goal is to enhance the readability of the text by making it easier for the reader's eye to move down the narrow column quickly and easily. Justifying keeps the text inside the boundaries of the column.

In the Bible sense of the word, justification means keeping one's behaviors within the boundaries that produce God's blessing. To be justified means that a person has been placed within the "column" of God's forgiveness, blessing, and favor, and therefore is not subject to condemnation. Justification occurs in the life of the Christian on the basis of what Jesus accomplished on the cross and what the person has believed—that Jesus is the Savior.

James wrote, "a man is justified by works, and not by faith only." The image is that of a person's life—as a living letter of God's mercy and grace—being bordered on the one side by faith and on the other side by works. The two together create the "column" in which a person's life flows in a focused, meaningful expression of what it means to be a Christian.

To have life framed only by faith means to have a ragged right column, open to all sorts of variation of what it means to manifest behavior that warrants God's blessing. To have life framed only by works means to have a ragged left column, and being open to false beliefs. It takes both good believing and good works for a person to remain "justified."

How does this word justification apply in practical ways to your life?

What do you envision life would be like if you only had to believe correctly and could do whatever you pleased?

What do you envision life would be like if you only had to do the right things, regardless of what you believed?

How does an interrelated balance of faith and works keep your Christian life and witness focused and intentional?

S
Supplementary Scriptures to Consider

James not only cited Abraham as a man of both faith and works, but Rahab of Jericho:

> Likewise, was not Rahab the harlot also justified by works when she received the messengers and sent them out another way?
>
> For as the body without the spirit is dead, so faith without works is dead also. (James 2:25–26)

- Reread Joshua 2 and 6. Rahab made a great faith statement, found in Joshua 2:11, "The LORD your God, He is God in heaven above and on earth beneath." But it was Rahab's actions based upon her belief in the sovereignty of God that justified her when Jericho was conquered by the Israelites. How did faith and works go together in Rahab's life?

- James seemed to teach that faith dies within a person if it does not find a practical outflow of expression. Do you agree or disagree with that assessment? Why so?

- How has faith become strengthened through works in your life? Has your faith grown the more you have become involved in sharing your faith with others, in words and through practical service? How so?

James also had this to say about good works:

> Therefore, to him who knows to do good and does not do it, to him it is sin. (James 4:17)

• In what ways does a failure to do the good works a person knows to do result in a person missing the mark of God's perfect plan?

• The early church fathers spoke of sins of commission (things done) and sins of omission (things left undone). Identify several examples of sins of omission. Are these sins just as *willful* as sins of commission?

Jesus combined faith and works in his criticism of the scribes and Pharisees:

> "Woe to you, scribes and Pharisees, hypocrites! For you pay tithe of mint and anise and cummin, and have neglected the weightier matters of the law: justice and mercy and faith. These you ought to have done, without leaving the others undone. (Matthew 23:23)

• Jesus criticized the religious leaders of his day for emphasizing works—in this case, the tithing of herbs from their gardens—and ignoring faith. James admonishes a church rich in faith not to ignore works! Are faith and works equally important? Why might a person or a church gravitate more to one or the other when allocating time, curriculum, or resources?

• Do you believe your church places greater emphasis on faith or works? Do you personally place higher value on one or the other?

I

Introspection and Implications

1. James wrote, "By works faith was made perfect." The word *perfect* refers to being made whole or completed. In what ways have you discovered that works complete your faith?

2. Do you believe that both faith and works are necessary for a genuine Christian life? Why?

3. In what ways does the meeting of earthly needs enhance the meeting of eternal needs?

4. James pointed to Abraham and his obedience in sacrificing Isaac as an example of faith and works joined together. James asked rhetorically, "Do you see that faith was working together with his works, and by works faith was made perfect?" How do *you* answer James' question?

5. Respond to these statements made by James: "You believe that there is one God. You do well. Even the demons believe—and tremble!"

6. Are all good deeds examples of faith in action? Why or why not?

7. Do you feel guilty for not doing more good works? If so, why do you believe you feel this way? If not, why not?

C
Communicating the Good News

A number of Christian charitable organizations require those they help (usually with food and shelter) to hear a message that presents the Gospel of Jesus Christ. Is this a good or bad idea? Why?

To what extent and in what ways should a believer let a person know that he or she is giving their service, time, talents, or resources in the name of the Lord? Is there any difference in approach that we should take for the unsaved (or for the saved) person who needs assistance?

LESSON #4

POWER IN WHAT WE SAY

Defile: to corrupt or ruin, to make something sacred or holy no longer fit for use

B
Bible Focus

> *We all stumble in many things. If anyone does not stumble*
> *in word, he is a perfect man, able also to bridle the whole*
> *body. Indeed, we put bits in horses' mouths that they may obey*
> *us, and we turn their whole body. Look also at ships: although*
> *they are so large and are driven by fierce winds, they are*
> *turned by a very small rudder wherever the pilot desires. Even*
> *so the tongue is a little member and boasts great things.*
>
> *See how great a forest a little fire kindles! And the tongue is*
> *a fire, a world of iniquity. The tongue is so set among our*
> *members that it defiles the whole body, and sets on fire the*
> *course of nature; and it is set on fire by hell. For every kind of*
> *beast and bird, of reptile and creature of the sea, is tamed and*
> *has been tamed by mankind. But no man can tame the tongue.*
> *It is an unruly evil, full of deadly poison. With it we bless our*
> *God and Father, and with it we curse men, who have been*
> *made in the similitude of God. Out of the same mouth proceed*
> *blessing and cursing. My brethren, these things ought not to*
> *be so. Does a spring send forth fresh water and bitter from the*
> *same opening? Can a fig tree, my brethren, bear olives, or a*
> *grapevine bear figs? Thus no spring yields both salt water and*
> *fresh. (James 3:2–12)*

What a short course on the power of the spoken word! Everybody makes mistakes or slips up, James told the church, but the person who is truly complete in Christ does not stumble in what he says! In other words, to be "perfect" or mature in the Christian life, people must give tremendous care to their speech.

James went on to make these points:

First, the person who is able to control his tongue is able to manage every other aspect of his life. The implication is clear: the most difficult aspect of our lives to control is our speech. Discipline regarding speech is the first and foremost discipline.

Second, a person is prone to overstate her own goodness. Our speech is usually the first indicator of pride. Perhaps the greatest statement of pride is this: "I have no sin, and therefore, I have no need to repent of sin or receive forgiveness from God for sin." The New Testament writers stand squarely against such thinking. Paul wrote to the Romans, "There is none righteous, no, not one. For all have sinned and fall short of the glory of God" (Romans 3:10, 23). John wrote, "If we say that we have no sin, we deceive ourselves, and the truth is not in us" (1 John 1:8). The Book of Ecclesiastes says, "There is not a man on earth who does good and does not sin" (Ecclesiastes 7:20). Pride leads people to overestimate their importance in the church, their position among others, and their superiority of opinion and understanding. Pride usually begins and ends with the all-important "I." The proud person is known for saying, "I am," "I will," "I think," "I choose," "I know," "I decide," or "I have." Close behind are the words *me* and *my*.

Third, what we say defiles us—it produces corruption and ruin, within our individual selves and within the body of Christ as a whole. The word *defile* also refers to a holy or sacred vessel being rendered unclean for use in the service of God. What a person says can render a lifetime of witness for Christ Jesus null and void. Students of history know this has happened countless times in the history of the church, and in today's media world careless words can go around the world in a matter of minutes, effectively destroying years of ministry.

Fourth, it is easier to *slip up*—which is the word translated as sin in this passage—in our speech than in any other area of behavior. The careless slip of the tongue generally happens when we are taken off guard, are overly tired, or are careless and unintentional in what we say. There is no sin that is easier to commit, and none that has more far-reaching consequences.

James also confronted a frequently held concept that it is entirely acceptable for a person to speak both evil and good, since every person is both evil and good in varying degrees. Such dualism within a Christian is neither warranted nor acceptable. The New Testament consistently states that at the moment of spiritual conversion a sinner becomes a newborn saint. He becomes a new creature in quality, not merely proportionately less a sinner. There is no sliding scale of behavior between righteous and unrighteous. A person in right standing with God will speak what is good. A person who is not in right standing with God will speak evil. There should be no tolerance for careless speech that promotes evil. Period.

Finally, James used three metaphors in his teaching about the power of spoken words. They are like:

- *a bit in a horse's mouth*—the tongue gives direction to life—it is a precursor of what we will choose to do. What we say moves us to action.

- *the small rudder of a great ship*—even in the face of great crisis, spoken words can establish a course of action that withstands or confronts a difficult circumstance.

- *a fire*—words of criticism, gossip, and false teaching can spread like wildfire in a body of believers. God's Word says, "An ungodly man digs up evil, and it is on his lips like a burning fire. A perverse man sows strife, and a whisperer separates the best of friends" (Proverbs 16:27–28).

Speech, in the end, is a barometer of spirituality. It reveals the heart. Those who are inconsistent and deceitful in belief or attitude will become inconsistent and deceitful in speech, and in turn will become inconsistent and deceitful in actions.

We must never merely "watch what we say" or "think before we speak," but, indeed, we must evaluate our thoughts, attitudes, beliefs, and feelings so that the *wellspring* of our speech is pure and godly.

What about this passage from James challenges *you* to reevaluate your own spoken words?

A
Application for Today

In all of biblical history, one of the most profound and passionate statements about the power of the spoken word is the one found below. The words are those of the Jewish writer Jesus ben Sirach, who believed the tongue had tremendous destructive potential. For the greatest impact, read the passage aloud, slowly and with emotion:

> Cursed be the whisperer and the double-tongued, for such have destroyed many who were at peace. A backbiting tongue has disquieted many and driven them from nation to nation—strong cities have been pulled down and the houses of great men overthrown. An evil tongue has cut in pieces the forces of people and undone strong nations. A backbiting tongue has cast out virtuous women and deprived them of their livelihood. Whoever hearkens to an evil tongue shall never find rest and never dwell quietly, neither shall he have a friend in whom he may repose.
>
> The stroke of the whip makes marks in the flesh, but the stroke of the tongue breaks bones. Many have fallen by the edge of the sword, but not as many as have fallen by the tongue. Well is he who is defended from an evil tongue and has not passed through its venom, who has not drawn its yoke, nor been bound in its bands. For the yoke of an evil tongue is a yoke of iron and the bands of it are bands of brass. The death of an evil tongue is an evil death—the grave is better than living in its presence.

Look at how you hedge your possessions about with
thorns and bind up your silver and gold, and in like manner,
weigh your words in a balance and make a bridle for your
lips and make a door and a bar for your mouth. Beware that
you do not slide by it, lest you fall before the one who lies in
wait for you and experience a fall that is incurable and leads
to death. (Ecclesiasticus 28).

Do we tend to dismiss the power of the spoken word today? Or, do we
over-exaggerate the power of words?

Are we so bombarded by words that we no longer feel the full force of
their power? Do words still mean something?

Do we as a society place greater emphasis on glibness of speech or
well-measured words?

Do we as a society have tolerance for speech-making that is longer than a
sound bite?

Do you sometimes take in words without realizing their power to alter
your perceptions, attitudes, and beliefs? Are you ever in danger of being led
astray by empty speech without realizing what is happening to you?

Is Jesus ben Sirach right about speech in <u>our</u> day?

S
Supplementary Scriptures to Consider

James warned teachers, who conveyed their messages, to a great extent,
by the spoken word:

My brethren, let not many of you become teachers, knowing
that we shall receive a stricter judgment. (James 3:1)

• Have you ever taught—any subject at any level? Then you likely know
how easy it is to say something that is not completely accurate or loving
in the heat of the moment? How can a person guard against this?

- Why do you believe that teachers receive a "stricter judgment"? Is there a different standard for those who speak with authority and before an audience and those who are speaking in normal conversation?

- Very often we judge those who speak publicly or from positions of authority according to their speaking abilities more than for the accuracy of their message. Why is it important in the church to have teachers who weigh their words carefully and speak with the intent to convey the "whole truth and nothing but the truth"?

James advised those in the church to place greater emphasis on hearing than on speaking:

> So then, my beloved brethren, let every man be swift to hear, slow to speak, slow to wrath; for the wrath of man does not produce the righteousness of God. (James 1:19–20)

- What does it mean to you for a person to be "swift to hear"?

• What does it mean for a person to be "slow to speak"?

• How is this admonition regarding communication related to being "slow to wrath"?

• Can you recall an incident in your life when you spoke too rashly or too quickly? What happened?

James linked unbridled speech with deceit:

> If anyone among you thinks he is religious, and does not bridle his tongue but deceives his own heart, this one's religion is useless. (James 1:26)

• What does it mean to you to bridle the tongue? How does a person do this in a practical way?

• How is bridling the tongue related to deceit of the heart?

James addressed an issue that was common to those from a Jewish background— the adding of an "oath" to underscore the importance of their words:

> Above all, my brethren, do not swear, either by heaven or by earth or with any other oath. But let your "Yes" be "Yes," and your "No," "No," lest you fall into judgment. (James 5:12)

• Why would adding of oaths lead a person to fall into judgment?

• Compare this statement in James to what Jesus said as part of the Sermon on the Mount: "Again you have heard that it was said to those of old, 'You shall not swear falsely, but shall perform your oaths to the Lord.'

But I say to you, do not swear at all: neither by heaven, for it is God's throne; nor by the earth, for it is His footstool; nor by Jerusalem, for it is the city of the great King. Nor shall you swear by your head, because you cannot make one hair white or black. But let your 'Yes' be 'Yes,' and your 'No,' 'No.' For whatever is more than these is from the evil one." (Matthew 5:33–37) Jesus pointed out that people were adding oaths to give greater strength or importance to their words and swearing that those words were backed up by things of great importance and an unchanging nature. But in truth they were swearing by things that were not rightfully theirs! In other words, they were claiming a right of privilege to use things that belonged to God or were solely under God's authority. Only a person's word is truly owned by that individual. How does this add meaning to what James said about oaths being subject to judgment?

• What do you say to add greater weight to promises, assurances, or answers related to fact and opinion? Do you use additional words?

Jesus placed great importance on accuracy and veracity of the spoken word:

> Jesus said: "I say to you that for every idle word men may speak, they will give account of it in the day of judgment. For by your words you will be justified, and by your words you will be condemned." (Matthew 12:36–37)

• How do you define "every idle word"?

• In what way do your words justify you or condemn you?

The Book of Proverbs has a great deal to say about communication, including these words of wisdom:

> A soft answer turns away wrath,
> But a harsh word stirs up anger.
> The tongue of the wise uses knowledge rightly,
> But the mouth of fools pours forth foolishness.
> A wholesome tongue is a tree of life,
> But perverseness in it breaks the spirit. (Proverbs 15:1–2, 4)

• How does this passage relate to what James wrote about the spoken word and wrath?

• What stands out to you in a special way in this passage from Proverbs? Is there an area of your own communication that you need to address?

I
Introspection and Implications

1. What about your personal communication would you like to change the most? How do you believe you should go about making that change?

2. In what ways do you find it difficult to monitor your speech?

3. In what ways is it difficult to receive admonition from others regarding your words or the ways in which you communicate?

4. Have you ever been the victim of malicious gossip? How did you respond, inwardly as well as outwardly?

5. Have you ever been taught an error, intentionally or unintentionally? How did you respond (inwardly and outwardly) when you learned it was incorrect?

C
Communicating the Good News

What do you believe to be the link between the teaching of James on the power of the tongue and evangelism ?

LESSON #5

WISDOM IN RELATIONSHIPS

*Partiality: an unfair preference for one
person or thing over another*

B
Bible Focus

> *If you really fulfill the royal law according to the Scripture,*
> *"You shall love your neighbor as yourself," you do well; but if*
> *you show partiality, you commit sin, and are convicted by the*
> *law as transgressors. For whoever shall keep the whole law,*
> *and yet stumble in one point, he is guilty of all. For He who*
> *said, "Do not commit adultery," also said, "Do not murder."*
> *Now if you do not commit adultery, but you do murder, you*
> *have become a transgressor of the law. So speak and so do as*
> *those who will be judged by the law of liberty. For judgment is*
> *without mercy to the one who has shown no mercy. Mercy*
> *triumphs over judgment. (James 2:8–13)*

Class distinctions were just as common, or more so, in the first century as today. Generally speaking, there were few who could be considered middle class. The two main categories of people were rich and poor. James and other writers in the New Testament called upon Christians to ignore social distinctions and to remember that the kingdom of heaven belonged to those who were "poor in spirit," not to those rich or poor in possessions. Jesus had clearly taught, "You shall love your neighbor as yourself" (Matthew 22:39).

What many Christians do not recognize is that this command to love your neighbor as yourself was at the heart of the Old Testament law. The first five books of the Old Testament are considered the books of the law." Originally, these five books were regarded as one long and undivided teaching. The division into distinct books came about because scrolls had a limited length. If all of the words of these five books are considered, the words that are at the center of the law are the words in Leviticus 19. This chapter repeats portions of the Ten Commandments about how to relate to God and to other people. In many ways James was paraphrasing a passage the Jews knew well:

> You shall do no injustice in judgment. You shall not be
> partial to the poor, nor honor the person of the mighty. In
> righteousness you shall judge your neighbor. You shall not
> go about as a talebearer among your people; nor shall you
> take a stand against the life of your neighbor: I am the LORD.
> You shall not hate your brother in your heart. You shall
> surely rebuke your neighbor, and not bear sin because of
> him. You shall not take vengeance, nor bear any grudge
> against the children of your people, but you shall love your
> neighbor as yourself: I am the LORD. (Leviticus 19:15–18)

The law of Moses stood squarely against showing partiality of any kind when it came to extending the mercy of God. To break any aspect of the Law was to break the whole of the Law. Keeping the Law, of course, was a requirement for holiness—to be set apart from evil and for good as God's people. Leviticus 19 begins, "You shall be holy for I the LORD your God am holy" (vs. 2).

The Law dealt with extremely practical matters—the reaping of harvests, stealing, lying, cheating and robbing neighbors by withholding wages, mistreating the blind and lame, showing partiality in rendering legal judgments, gossiping against others, refraining from rebuking an errant brother or sister, showing vengeance, bearing grudges, and so forth. In these practical ways, the Israelites were admonished to refrain from all partiality.

To be partial toward another person does not mean that you cannot *like* one person more than another. Nor does it mean that you cannot become better friends with some people or families in the church than with others. It means, rather, that we must not give favor to any person when it comes to what we give to them or require of them against the standard of God's Word. In other words, we cannot treat one person with greater kindness or forgiveness. We must never evaluate sin and righteousness according to our feelings. All must be treated with equity before the throne of God.

How difficult is it to refrain from partiality?

In what ways does a church suffer when partiality exists?

In what ways is a church blessed when partiality is replaced with equity before God?

A
Application for Today

A woman called her sister to describe a series of events for wives who were attending an executive corporate conference with their husbands. The wives had come from across the nation. Given their husband's positions and income levels, they were women who most people would describe as wealthy. They certainly were people who knew what it was like to be married to a man who traveled a great deal and very likely spent long hours at work and away from their family. Most were well-educated. The sister said, "You must have had a great time!"

"Not really," the sister said. "Most of the women just weren't my type."

"But it would seem you had a lot in common with them," the woman replied.

"Everything but Christ Jesus," the sister said. "I feel guilty for not sharing more about Christ, but it is difficult for me to know what to do in that environment, especially where my husband's career is involved."

"Are you talking about witnessing about Jesus as the Savior?" the woman asked.

"Yes, but not just that," her sister said. "Jesus taught that we are to love our neighbors as ourselves. I struggle in loving these women. I struggle in my attitude toward them and my judgment of them. I ask myself often, 'Are these women really my neighbors?' or are my neighbors the women in my church. I don't seem to have any difficulty relating to the women in my church—poor as well as rich—but what about those who don't know Christ?"

How would you answer the questions this woman posed?

Do you struggle with Jesus' command to "love your neighbor as your-self"?

Do you find it easy to show partiality to those you like and admire, or to those who are of like faith, whether in the church or outside the church?

In what ways is it difficult to treat everyone alike before the Lord?

S
Supplementary Scriptures to Consider

James described an example of partiality in the early church:

> My brethren, do not hold the faith of our Lord Jesus Christ,
> the Lord of glory, with partiality. For if there should come into
> your assembly a man with gold rings, in fine apparel, and
> there should also come in a poor man in filthy clothes, and
> you pay attention to the one wearing the fine clothes and say
> to him, "You sit here in a good place," and say to the poor
> man, "You stand there," or, "Sit here at my footstool," have
> you not shown partiality among yourselves, and become
> judges with evil thoughts? (James 2:1–4)

• Do you find it easier to openly accept a person into your circle of friends on the basis of what you perceive to be their socioeconomic status? What about accepting a person into your church as a member? What about accepting a person fully at church functions, on committees, and as a participant in various ministries?

- What do you look for when you first see another person? Do you evaluate people according to their clothing or jewelry?

- Do you seek out or shun certain people at a church service or social function, choosing to speak to some and sit with various ones, while avoiding others? Is this unintentional or intentional? Is there a difference in judgment according to whether a person's response is intentional or unintentional in these matters?

- What do we seek to gain through affiliating with others of higher socioeconomic status? What do we fear we will lose if we affiliate with others of lower socioeconomic status?

James had harsh words toward those who were rich and didn't use their wealth to help others.

> Listen, my beloved brethren: Has God not chosen the poor of
> this world to be rich in faith and heirs of the kingdom which
> He promised to those who love Him? But you have dishon-
> ored the poor man. Do not the rich oppress you and drag you
> into the courts? Do they not blaspheme that noble name by
> which you are called? (James 2:5–7)

• Do you believe the poor are automatically "heirs of the kingdom"? If not, in what way did James define poor? (See Jesus' words in Matthew 5:3, "Blessed are the poor in spirit, for theirs is the kingdom of heaven.")

• Do you believe the poor in money are automatically rich in faith? In what ways might material impoverishment cause a person to become stronger in faith? Are all people required to divest themselves of external wealth as a part of becoming "rich in faith"? Does this passage refer only to those who are poor in spirit?

- Have you ever experienced mistreatment at the hand of a wealthy person? Did you perceive that the mistreatment was the result of their wealth? What happened? Are there character traits that wealthy people automatically display? Are there character traits a wealthy person must guard against developing? Are these traits unique to the wealthy?

James also spelled out what it means to have a self-seeking attitude and the ways in which such an attitude is linked to partiality:

> Who is wise and understanding among you? Let him show by good conduct that his works are done in the meekness of wisdom. But if you have bitter envy and self-seeking in your hearts, do not boast and lie against the truth. This wisdom does not descend from above, but is earthly, sensual, demonic. For where envy and self-seeking exist, confusion and every evil thing are there, But the wisdom that is from above is first pure, then peaceable, gentle, willing to yield, full of mercy and good fruits, without partiality and without hypocrisy. Now the fruit of righteousness is sown in peace by those who make peace. (James 3:13–18)

- Have you ever experienced a situation in which envy and self-seeking attitudes caused "confusion and every evil thing"? What happened?

- In what ways do we each find it difficult to own up to our own envy and self-seeking attitudes, even to the point of claiming that we do not have any envy and that all of our motives are pure?

- James used several adjectives to describe the wisdom that comes from God. Respond to each of these by defining them in practical terms related to daily living:

    Pure:

    Peaceable:

    Gentle:

    Willing to yield:

    Full of mercy and good fruits:

    Without partiality and hypocrisy:

• What does it mean to you that the "fruit of righteousness" is "sown in peace by those who make peace"? How does this relate to Jesus' teaching, "Blessed are the peacemakers, for they shall be called sons of God" (Matthew 5:9)? Does this mean that peace must be achieved by peaceful means in order for the fruit to be in God's will? Are non-peaceful means ever acceptable?

James described words against a fellow Christian as a violation of God's law:

> Do not speak evil of one another, brethren. He who speaks evil of a brother and judges his brother, speaks evil of the law and judges the law. But if you judge the law, you are not a doer of the law but a judge. There is one Lawgiver, who is able to save and to destroy. Who are you to judge another?
> (James 4:11–12)

• What does it mean to you to "speak evil" of a fellow believer?

• A person has said, "We are to judge behavior, not people." What does this statement mean to you?

• Some in the early church were seeking to adjust the law, claiming that it was too harsh. Have you seen evidence of this in today's church? Can a person ever fully obey something that he believes to be partially untrue or partially inapplicable?

James made a distinction between speaking evil of another person and grumbling against one another:

> Do not grumble against one another, brethren, lest you be condemned. Behold, the Judge is standing at the door! My brethren, take the prophets, who spoke in the name of the Lord, as an example of suffering and patience. Indeed we count them blessed who endure. You have heard of the perseverance of Job and seen the end intended by the Lord—that the Lord is very compassionate and merciful. (James 5:9–11)

• Define *grumble* in your own words. What does it mean to you, in practical terms, to grumble against another person?

- James cited very specific words to those who are patient with others, even in times of suffering. How can you use the words of the prophets to encourage others?

- In what ways is it difficult to persevere and be patient with people whom you believe might be contributing to your suffering?

I
Introspection and Implications

1. Does a person automatically show partiality any time he criticizes another person?

2. In what ways do you find it difficult to refrain from all partiality, including the difficulty of *recognizing* when you are feeling or showing partiality?

3. What do we gain by associating with people who are not just like us—racially, in socioeconomic status, in background, in culture?

4. If we are to treat all people with equity before the law, is there a distinction in showing partiality to those who do not break the law? Is there any person who is truly innocent before the standard of the law? In what ways might James have been calling the church to recognize that all are sinners (lawbreakers) in need of a Savior?

5. What does it mean to be *fair* to other people?

6. Is there a difference between "being partial" and "preferring"? If so, what is the difference?

C
Communicating the Good News

Is there automatic partiality that believers show other Christians, as opposed to those who do not believe? In what ways are we to love all people equally? Are there ways in which we are to express special love for those who are fellow Christians?

LESSON #6

CONFRONTING SELF

*Enmity: extreme ill will or
hatred between enemies*

B
Bible Focus

> *Where do wars and fights come from among you? Do they*
> *not come from your desires for pleasure that war in your*
> *members? You lust and do not have. You murder and covet and*
> *cannot obtain. You fight and war. Yet you do not have because*
> *you do not ask. You ask and do not receive, because you ask*
> *amiss, that you may spend it on your pleasures. Adulterers and*
> *adulteresses! Do you not know that friendship with the world*
> *is enmity with God? Whoever therefore wants to be a friend of*
> *the world makes himself an enemy of God. Or do you think*
> *that the Scripture says in vain, "The Spirit who dwells in us*
> *yearns jealously"?*
> *But He gives more grace. Therefore He says:*
> *"God resists the proud,*
> *But gives grace to the humble."*
> *Therefore submit to God. Resist the devil and he will flee*
> *from you. Draw near to God and He will draw near to you.*
> *Cleanse your hands, you sinners; and purify your hearts, you*
> *double-minded. Lament and mourn and weep! Let your*
> *laughter be turned to mourning and your joy to gloom.*
> *Humble yourselves in the sight of the Lord, and He will lift*
> *you up. (James 4:1–10)*

James covered a number of subjects in just a few verses, but if one steps
back just a little from these seemingly diverse topics, a central word
emerges: *self*.

Self's lust for pleasure generates envy and greed, which in turn are key
factors in creating conflicts. It is conflict between individuals that easily
escalates into struggles within families and organizations, including the
church. Such conflicts, if left unchecked, can ultimately produce wars among
nations.

Putting *self* first keeps a person from asking God for the necessary things
of life. A proud person generally believes he or she can accomplish all that is
needed to sustain life or achieve a higher quality of life.

Putting *self*'s desires at the center of one's prayers is a prime reason for
not receiving what is requested from God.

A preoccupation with *self* leads a person to believe in humanism, which
contends that humanity can solve its own problems through human wisdom
and compassion.

An exaltation of *self* denies God His rightful place in a person's life. It
should be noted that the reference to adulterers and adulteresses in this

passage refers to spiritual adultery—a person's turning from God as the true husband of His beloved people.

Self equates to pride. It is *self*-first pride in people that causes God to withhold the fullness of His blessing.

For people to truly be lifted up by God in this life, they must first deny *self*. They must humble themselves before God, purify their hearts of selfish motives and desires, and submit to God's way rather than their own way.

Few things are simpler to understand and more difficult to <u>do</u>!

Looking at this passage from a different perspective, one can find clear answers to some of life's most demanding questions:

- What causes war?
- What causes dissension within a family, community, or nation?
- What keeps a person from fully receiving what is truly necessary?
- What keeps prayers from being answered?
- What causes a person to fall short of all God desires to give?

In most cases, if we want to encounter our own worst enemy we only need to look in a mirror. Even so, pride is the most difficult of all attributes for a person to detect in himself or herself. We rarely are willing to own up to pride in even small quantities!

In your personal life, what do you perceive to be your foremost issues related to pride?

A
Application for Today

Have you ever noticed . . .

When ANOTHER person ignores you, he is rude. When YOU ignore him, you are preoccupied with something more important.

When ANOTHER person is set in his ways, he is obstinate. When YOU are set in your ways, you are being consistent and following your convictions?

When ANOTHER person doesn't like one of your friends, he is prejudiced or bigoted. When YOU don't like one of their friends, you are a good judge of character.

When ANOTHER person is mild-mannered, he is weak. When YOU are mild-mannered, you are gracious.

When ANOTHER person says what he thinks, he is opinionated and spiteful. When YOU say what you think, you are being frank and open.

When ANOTHER person dresses extravagantly or in expensive garments, he is being ostentatious. When YOU dress in your finest, you are showing your good sense of style.

When ANOTHER person turns out to have foretold what happens, he is a good guesser. When YOU turn out to be right about events as they unfold, you are discerning.

When ANOTHER person speaks to you about your pride, he is being arrogant and unkind. When YOU speak to another person about her pride, you are being helpful and godly.

When ANOTHER person receives an abundance of provision, he is lucky. When YOU receive an abundance, you are worthy.

When ANOTHER person has a prayer answered, God is being merciful. When YOU have a prayer answered, God is being just.

How difficult is it for us to see ourselves as we are?

S
Supplementary Scriptures to Consider

James also had this to say about those who put *self* at the center of all their planning:

> Come now, you who way, "Today or tomorrow we will go to such and such a city, spend a year there, buy and sell, and make a profit"; whereas you do not know what will happen tomorrow. For what is your life? It is even a vapor that appears for a little time and then vanishes away. Instead you ought to say, "If the Lord wills, we shall live and do this or that." But now you boast in your arrogance. All such boasting is evil. (James 4:13–16)

• Who is ultimately in charge of what a person *can* do? Who is responsible for what *will* be accomplished or done?

• What is God's role when it comes to our dreams, goals, and plans? What is our part in dreaming, setting goals, and planning?

• How do you personally go about discerning what plans you make for yourself and your family? How do you set goals within specified time frames?

The Book of Proverbs has much to say about the humble and the proud. Consider this passage:

> Surely He scorns the scornful,
> But gives grace to the humble.
> The wise shall inherit glory,
> But shame shall be the legacy of fools. (Proverbs 3:35)

• To be scornful is to express contempt, considering something to be worthless, inferior, or undeserving of respect. Have you ever been the object of scorn? How did you respond, inwardly and outwardly?

- To be humble is to be unassuming or modest in attitude and behavior. It also means showing respect and deference to other people. Have you ever been around a person you believed was truly humble? How did that person make you feel? Did their humility and deference irritate you or cause you to feel admiration? How did you respond to that person?

Jesus taught this:

> "If anyone desires to come after Me, let him deny himself, and take up his cross, and follow Me. For whoever desires to save his life will lose it, but whoever loses his life for My sake will find it." (Matthew 16:24–25)

- What does it mean for you personally to deny self and follow Christ?

- What do we lose in placing supreme importance on *self*? What do we gain in placing supreme importance on *self*?

I
Introspection and Implications

1. Respond to this statement made by James: "Whoever wants to be a friend of the world makes himself an enemy of God" (James 4:4). What does it mean to be a "friend of the world"? How can we guard ourselves against adopting the perspective and belief system of the world? To what extent can believers in Christ Jesus be genuine *friends* with sinners? (Note: You may need to define genuine friendship.)

2. James made two brief but tremendous statements: "Submit to God. Resist the devil and he will flee from you" (James 4:7). To submit is to obey or become subject to another person. James also said, "Draw near to God and He will draw near to you" (James 4:8).

   • How do you submit to God in practical ways? How do you draw near to God in practical ways? Do submitting and drawing near involve only a change of attitude, or do these terms also involve behavior? How do you experience God drawing closer to you when you draw close to Him?

• How do you resist the devil in practical ways? How have you experienced the devil fleeing from you when you resist him?

C
Communicating the Good News

If all that a sinner knows is *self* —and a lifetime of meeting *self*'s needs and doing what is pleasing to *self* —how does a person intent on evangelism best convey the concepts of denying self and following Christ?

"Most of the wars in this world are over religion. I want peace, not war. I'd rather not be religious and live in peace than be religious and fight." What do you say to an unbeliever who presents this line of argument?

LESSON #7

HEALING FOR ALL WHO ARE SUFFERING

Fervent: so hot it glows; showing ardent or extremely passionate enthusiasm

B
Bible Focus

> *Is anyone among you suffering? Let him pray. Is anyone*
> *cheerful? Let him sing psalms. Is anyone among you sick? Let*
> *him call for the elders of the church, and let them pray over*
> *him, anointing him with oil in the name of the Lord. And the*
> *prayer of faith will save the sick, and the Lord will raise him*
> *up. And if he has committed sins, he will be forgiven. Confess*
> *your trespasses to one another, and pray for one another, that*
> *you may be healed. The effective, fervent prayer of a righteous*
> *man avails much. Elijah was a man with a nature like ours,*
> *and he prayed earnestly that it would not rain; and it did not*
> *rain on the land for three years and six months. And he prayed*
> *again, and the heaven gave rain, and the earth produced its*
> *fruit.* (James 5:13–18)

If you had to sum up the foremost characteristics of the early church in four action-packed words, those four words might very well be these:

- **Praying**—those in the early church were quick to take their needs to God. They petitioned God frequently for His presence, provision, and protection. Prayer was considered the first recourse, not the last resort, in times of trouble or suffering.

The admonition to all believers everywhere: *When you suffer, pray!*

- **Singing**—the early church was a people who readily offered praise to God, often set to music. *Psalms* are *songs*. Many of the psalms include admonitions to rejoice before the Lord and sing to the glory of His name.

The admonition to all believers everywhere*: When you are blessed, praise!*

- **Healing**—the early church regarded a person as an entity unable to be divided or fragmented—a being with physical, spiritual, emotional, and mental capacities that exist simultaneously and are interrelated in mysterious ways. Disease and injury impacted the *whole* of a person. In like manner, if one person was sick in the body of Christ, which is the church, then the whole body was impacted. Therefore, in times of illness—whether physical, emotional, or spiritual—the sick were encouraged to call upon others in the body to pray for them with faith, anointing them with oil in the name of the Lord. This was not an application of oil symbolically preparing a person for death but, rather, an active application of oil to a person's body. Very often the laying on of hands was something of a medicinal massage using a mix of herbs and pure olive oil. In the earliest church documents are records that command at least one widow in a church to be responsible for healing the women, and that male deacons were to be skilled in healing men. It should be noted that the Hebrew root word for both save and heal is the same. The Jewish believers had a firm understanding that God saved the entirety of a person, not just the spirit. Any sins that were related to a sickness were to be forgiven or loosed and set free as part of the prayers.

The admonition to all believers everywhere: *When you are sick, call upon others to pray for you and with you.*

- **Confessing**—the early church had a strong awareness that when one person trespassed against another, the whole of the body of Christ was tainted. The Bible has a number of words for sin, and trespass refers to a sin that is against another person. In today's language we might say, "When you hurt another person, go to that person and make amends and pray for each other to restore your relationship."

The admonition to all believers everywhere: *When you trespass against someone in the church, quickly confess your trespass to that person, pray together, and restore your relationship in Christ Jesus!*

James believed the *fervent* prayers of individual believers—"glowing hot in godly passion"—were effective in bringing about change, including changes in the natural order. If the earnest prayers of a human being such as Elijah could start and stop a drought, James had no doubt that earnest faith-filled prayer could bring about an end to suffering and start the flow of healing and forgiveness in the church!

Do you believe as James believed?

A
Application for Today

One of the most famous statements about prayer in the English language is the one below penned by the famous English poet Alfred Lord Tennyson:

"More things are wrought by prayer
Than this world dreams of. Wherefore, let thy voice
Rise like a fountain for me night and day.
For what are men better than sheep or goats
That nourish a blind life within the brain,

If, knowing God, they lift not hands of prayer
Both for themselves and those who call them friend?
For so the whole round earth is every way
Bound by gold chains about the feet of God."

A teacher once told his congregation: "It will not be until eternity that we truly know all of the ways that God has answered our prayers. This should not discourage us from praying but, rather, encourage us to pray all the more. We are part of a great and divine mystery. God has invited us to have a part in His ongoing and unfolding pageantry of meeting needs, alleviating suffering, saving souls, and working miracles. We no doubt are kept from seeing the full scope of our value in prayer or the full outcome of our intercession, lest we become proud and think that the work is related to our worthiness. Nonetheless, we are challenged to *keep on praying* in the same way that a generator keeps producing electricity without knowing all of the homes that are lit and all the work that is accomplished from the energy produced. God invites us to pray as a means of asking for God's intervention in our world. It is a surrender of our will so we can experience the full potential of His will. What awesome and privileged work it is to pray, never doubting but believing always that the God who calls us to pray both hears and answers. His answers pour to earth from eternity and, thus, are always far more than we can ask or comprehend. We do not need to know the precise answer to know that the answer has been precisely applied by a loving God."

Take time to consider carefully the above statements. Is there a concept that stands out to you in a special way? Do you believe the Lord is calling upon you to change something about the way you pray?

S
Supplementary Scriptures to Consider

The apostle Paul wrote this to the Corinthians about order in their church meetings:

> Whenever you come together, each of you has a psalm . . . let
> all things be done for edification. (1 Corinthians 14:26)

• Many churches begin their worship services with singing. What do you believe the benefits to be in approaching God first with praise and thanksgiving?

• How does praise music build up (edify) a person in faith and prepare that person to hear God's Word and pray?

• The psalms have this overriding characteristic: they point toward the greatness and glory of God over all earthly situations and human circumstances. What is your favorite praise song? Does it direct your heart and mind to the greatness and glory of God?

James concluded his letter with these words:

> Brethren, if anyone among you wanders from the truth, and someone turns him back, let him know that he who turns a sinner from the error of his way will save a soul from death and cover a multitude of sins. (James 5:19–20)

• How does this passage relate to praying for one another with faith to save the sick and to bring about reconciliation in the wake of confession of trespasses?

James referred to the prophet Elijah as a role model when it comes to earnest prayer. Reread the story of Elijah in 1 Kings 17 and 18. Note especially these verses that come after Elijah's showdown with the prophets of Baal:

> Then Elijah said to [King] Ahab, "Go up, eat and drink; for there is the sound of abundance of rain."
> So Ahab went up to eat and drink. And Elijah went up to the top of Carmel: then he bowed down on the ground, and put his face between his knees,
> and said to his servant, "Go up now, look toward the sea." So he went up and looked, and said, "There is nothing." And seven times he said, "Go again."
> Then it came to pass the seventh time, that he said, "There is a cloud, as small as a man's hand, rising out of the sea!" So he said, "Go up, say to Ahab, 'Prepare your chariot, and go down before the rain stops you.'" (1 Kings 18:41–44)

• Note that Elijah knew the sound of rain even before he prayed. How important is it to believe you will receive an answer to your prayers even before you voice them?

• What is the message to you in this passage about the importance of persistence in prayer, even if you do not see immediate satisfying or encouraging results?

• For a man to put his face between his knees was an act of total submission and agonizing prayer. Have you ever prayed for something with such intensity? Was there a difference in the words you voiced? What was the outcome of your prayer? Why do you believe people rarely have this degree of fervency as they pray?

• Note that Elijah recognized that a fairly small cloud on the horizon was the sign that rain was, indeed, imminent. Would you have considered this to be a certain sign of rain? Why or why not? What do you look for after you pray? Do you look for a sign that God is answering your specific prayers in a specific way? Why or why not? What would a "yes" sign look like to you?

I
Introspection and Implications

1. Have you ever confessed your trespasses to another believer in the church and then prayed together for your relationship to be reconciled? What happened as a result?

2. When you have a need or are in trouble, is your first recourse to pray? Why or why not?

3. When you experience something good in your life, is your first recourse to praise God? Why or why not?

4. When you are sick (physically or emotionally) is your first recourse to call for members of your church to pray for you? Why or why not?

5. Would you describe your church as praying, singing, healing, and confessing? If not, why not? What descriptive terms would you use?

C
Communicating the Good News

How important is prayer to evangelism? Consider the best ways of

• praying before an evangelistic outreach or service

• praying during an evangelistic service (publicly or behind-the-scenes intercession)

• praying after an evangelistic service or outreach

How do *you* pray for unbelievers to be reached by what you say and do?

Note to Editor: James 5:19-20 is also used as a supplementary passage earlier in this book, but the application in this chapter is different.

NOTES TO LEADERS
OF SMALL GROUPS

As the leader of a small discussion group, think of yourself as a facilitator with three main roles:

- Get the discussion started.

- Involve every person in the group.

- Encourage an open, candid discussion that remains Bible-focused.

You certainly don't need to be the person with all the answers! In truth, much of your role is to be a person who asks questions:

- What really impacted you most in this lesson?

- Did you find a particular part of the lesson or a question troubling?

- Did you find a particular part of the lesson encouraging or insightful?

- Did you find a particular part of the lesson you'd like to explore further?

Express to the group at the outset of your study that your goal as a group is to gain new insights into God's Word. This is not the forum for defending a point of doctrine or a theological opinion. Stay focused on what God's Word says and means. The purpose of the study is also to share insights on how to apply God's Word to everyday life. *Every* person in the group can and should contribute. The collective wisdom that flows from Bible-focused discussion is often very rich and deep.

Seek to create an environment in which every member of the group feels free to ask questions of other members in order to gain greater understanding. Encourage the group members to voice their appreciation to one another for new insights gained and to be supportive of one another personally. Take the lead in doing this. Genuinely appreciate and value the contributions made by each person.

You may want to begin each study by having one or more members of the group read through the section provided under "Bible Focus." Ask the group specifically if it desires to discuss any of the questions under the "Application" section, the "Supplemental Scriptures" section, and the "Implications" and "Communicating the Gospel" sections. You do not need to bring closure—or come to a definitive conclusion or consensus—about any one question asked in this study. Rather, if the group does not have a satisfactory Bible-based answer to a question, then the group encourages them to engage in further "asking, seeking, and knocking" strategies to discover the answers! Remember the words of Jesus: "Ask, and it will be given to you, seek, and you will find; knock, and it will be opened to you. For everyone who asks receives, and he who seeks finds, and to him who knocks it will be opened" (Matt. 7:7–8).

Finally, open and close your study with prayer. Ask the Holy Spirit, whom Jesus called the Spirit of Truth, to guide your discussion and to reveal what is of eternal benefit to you individually and as a group. As you close your study, ask the Holy Spirit to seal to your remembrance what you have read and studied and to show you in the upcoming days, weeks, and months *ways* to apply what you have studied to your daily life and relationships.

General Themes for the Lessons

Each lesson in this study has one or more core themes. Continually pull the group back to these themes. You can do this by asking simple questions, such as, "How does that related to _____?" or "How does that help us better understand the concept of _____?" or "In what ways does that help us apply the principle of _____?"

A summary of general themes or concepts in each lesson is provided below:

Lesson #1
FACING TRIALS AND TEMPTATIONS
Growing through times of testing
Overcoming times of temptation

Lesson #2
BECOMING DOERS OF THE WORD
The link between believing and behaving
The perfect law of liberty

Lesson #3

THE RELATIONSHIP BETWEEN FAITH AND WORKS

The importance of faith to works

The importance of works to faith

Justification by works plus faith

What it means to have a fully alive faith

Lesson #4

POWER IN WHAT WE SAY

The power of the spoken word

How to take control of one's own speech

Lesson #5

WISDOM IN RELATIONSHIPS

Partiality

Refraining from prejudice or snobbishness

Loving others as you love yourself

Lesson #6

CONFRONTING SELF

Facing and overcoming pride

Getting to the root of conflicts

Getting to the root cause of unanswered prayer

Lesson #7

HEALING FOR ALL WHO ARE SUFFERING

Prayer in times of suffering or need

The power and value of praise

Praying for the sick to be healed

Confessing faults one to another

Fervent, earnest prayer

NOTES